MOTORSPORTS

Pro Stock Car Racing

by William P. Mara

Consultant:
Dean Case
Motorsports Hall of Fame of America

CAPSTONE BOOKS

an imprint of Capstone Press
Mankato, Minnesota

Capstone Books are published by Capstone Press
151 Good Counsel Drive, P.O. Box 669, Mankato, Minnesota 56002
http://www.capstone-press.com

Library of Congress Cataloging-in-Publication Data
Mara, W. P.
    Pro stock car racing/by William P. Mara
       p. cm.—(Motorsports)
    Includes bibliographical references (p. 46) and index.
    Summary: Introduces the sport of stock car racing including its history, various
special features of the cars, and qualifications of drivers and crews.
    ISBN 0-7368-0025-5
    1. NASCAR (Association)—Juvenile literature. 2. Stock car racing—United
States—Juvenile literature. [1. NASCAR (Association) 2. Stock car racing.] I. Title.
II. Series.
GV1029.9.S74M32 1999
796.72'0973—dc21   98-20865
                                                          CIP
                                                           AC

Editorial Credits
Michael Fallon, editor; Timothy Halldin, cover designer; Sheri Gosewisch,
  photo researcher

Photo Credits
Daytona Racing Archives, 6, 10, 13
Janine Pestel, 4, 14, 16, 24, 26, 37
Joseph Pestel, 31
Sportschrome USA/Ron McQueen, cover; V. Bucci, 20; Robert Tringali, 32, 42
Steve Mohlenkamp, 8, 34
Transparencies, Inc./Jane Faircloth, 22, 28
Unicorn Stock Photos/Doug Adams, 41
Visuals Unlimited/Gary W. Carter, 18, 38

2 3 4 5 6 04 03 02 01 00

Table of Contents

Chapter 1

Pro Stock Car Racing

Pro stock cars are racing cars that can reach speeds of more than 200 miles (322 kilometers) per hour. Racing teams build stock cars by hand. Expert racing mechanics use car parts from manufacturers. Mechanics modify the parts to give the stock cars power. To modify means to change something for a new purpose.

Stock cars are very expensive. They cost four or five times as much as ordinary cars to build.

Pro stock car racers drive cars on tracks in stadiums. These large oval structures hold thousands of spectators. The spectators watch the races from behind strong walls.

The best stock car racers compete in races organized by the National Association of Stock Car Automobile Racing (NASCAR). Between

Pro stock car racers drive cars on tracks in stadiums.

Between 30 and 45 racers compete in NASCAR races.

---

30 and 45 racers compete in NASCAR races.
Racers receive money and prizes from NASCAR
if they win races. Racers also collect points. The
racer with the most points becomes the racing
champion at the end of the season. The NASCAR
racing season lasts from February to November.

NASCAR
NASCAR is the largest stock car racing
organization in the world. It has sanctioned

stock car races since 1947. NASCAR's approval makes the races official. NASCAR makes rules for stock car racers and gives prize money and trophies to champion racers.

NASCAR holds most of its races in the United States. A few exhibition races have taken place in countries such as Japan and Australia. Exhibition races do not count in the points standings for the racing season. But NASCAR hopes the exhibition races will create interest in stock car racing in these countries.

Pro Stock Car Races and Rules

NASCAR has three professional racing classes that race in the United States. Winston Cup Series races take place on large race tracks. Racers drive from 400 to 600 miles (644 to 966 kilometers) during races on large oval tracks. Busch Series races often take place on smaller tracks than Winston Cup Series races. Busch Series racers drive from 200 to 300 miles (322 to 483 kilometers) on oval tracks. But some Busch Series races are the same length as Winston Cup Series races.

The Craftsman Truck Series is another kind of NASCAR race.

NASCAR also sanctions races for trucks. The Craftsman Truck Series races began in 1995. The racers drive in two 100-mile (161-kilometer) races. There is a halftime break between the two races for mechanics to work on the trucks.

Each stock car in a stock car race must follow NASCAR's rules. NASCAR makes rules concerning what kinds of parts cars can have. Stock cars cannot race in NASCAR races if they do not follow the rules.

NASCAR also makes rules concerning the size of tracks and length of races. It also decides how many racers may compete in pro stock car races.

NASCAR uses a point system to determine the racing champion for each year. At the end of the season, race organizers add up the points for each racer. The racer with the most points receives more than $2 million in prize money. Racers share this money with car owners and racing crews.

Racers earn points in several ways during races. The racer who takes first place receives 175 points. The second-place racer wins 170 points. The racers from third place onward each receive five fewer points than the racer who placed ahead of them. The driver who leads a race for the most laps receives another five points. Any driver who leads a race also receives five points.

Chapter 2

People began to race modern stock cars in the 1930s. Racers gathered at Daytona Beach, Florida, to race their cars on the sand. A man named Bill France went to Florida to watch the races. He was a race car driver and auto mechanic from Washington, D.C.

France liked the races. He raced stock cars in a few of the races. In 1938, France decided to organize a race with his own money. He worked hard to promote the race. He made people aware of the race by advertising in local newspapers.

After the race, France added up the money people paid to see the race. He had a small amount of money left after paying all the business costs. This was the first stock car

---

Stock car drivers raced in the sand at Daytona Beach in the 1930s, 1940s, and 1950s.

race in Daytona to make a profit. France became a full-time race organizer and promoter.

The Early Days of NASCAR

In 1947, France formed an official racing organization. He named the organization the National Association of Stock Car Automobile Racing. France became the first president of NASCAR in 1948. He was president for 24 years until he retired. In 1972, his son Bill France Jr. became president of NASCAR.

NASCAR made racing rules and sanctioned races. The organization also set goals for the sport of stock car racing. NASCAR race organizers wanted to make stock car racing popular. They wanted to hold races all over the country.

The first NASCAR races took place in southeastern states. But France worked hard to promote NASCAR races across the United States. In 1951, France organized a race in Detroit, Michigan. Detroit is the home of many U.S. car makers. France wanted the car

---

The first NASCAR races took place in southeastern states such as Virginia, North Carolina, and Florida.

manufacturers to notice the sport of stock car racing. He hoped manufacturers would give both money and support. His plan worked.

Since the 1950s, car manufacturers in Detroit have supported NASCAR. The manufacturers offer prize money for races and give advice to racing teams on how to build faster cars. They also help to improve the safety of the stock cars.

The Growth of NASCAR

NASCAR officials wanted to move stock car races to official race tracks. France helped build the Daytona International Speedway in 1959. He organized the first Daytona 500 race that year. The race was 500 miles (805 kilometers) long. Thousands of spectators attended the race.

NASCAR racing became very popular in the 1960s and 1970s. Fans came to watch famous racers such as Richard Petty, Cale Yarborough, and Bobby Allison. People also began watching NASCAR races on television.

Bill France helped to build the Daytona International Speedway in 1959.

Some women racers also have competed in NASCAR races. In 1982, Diane Teel was the first woman to race in a NASCAR race. Janet Guthrie, Patty Moise, Tammy Jo Kirk, and Shawna Robinson are well-known racers.

NASCAR has continued to help people build race tracks. About 40 major NASCAR race tracks and many smaller race courses exist in the United States. NASCAR organizes nearly 300 pro stock car races each year. Today, stock car races draw more people than any other sport in the United States.

Shawna Robinson is a well-known stock car racer.

Chapter 3

Pro Stock Car Parts

NASCAR wants racers to win because of their driving abilities. No racer should have an advantage over other racers because of the kinds of parts in their cars.

The parts that mechanics use to build pro stock cars must follow NASCAR rules. These rules make sure all stock cars have the same kinds of parts. The parts must come from factories that make ordinary cars. Mechanics can modify the parts on pro stock cars. But each stock car should be generally the same.

Exterior Parts

Manufacturers specially design the exterior parts of stock cars. The exterior parts are those on the outside of the car. The manufacturers want stock car exteriors to be strong and safe.

Manufacturers specially design the exterior parts of stock cars.

Smooth rubber tires help stock cars grip race tracks.

Stock car bodies are important exterior parts. The bodies can rip apart in accidents. Mechanics have to add other parts to stock cars to keep the racers from being crushed in accidents. Mechanics put strong roll cages and chassis under stock car bodies to protect stock car racers. A chassis is a frame that supports the body of a stock car. A roll cage is a structure of strong metal tubing in stock cars that surrounds stock car racers.

Stock cars have strong axles in the rear. Axles are rods that connect to the center of wheels. Stock cars also have very strong suspension systems. These systems of shock absorbers connect each wheel to the body of a car. The strong suspension helps a driver control the car when traveling at high speeds over bumps.

A stock car has wide tires. The rubber tires are sticky and smooth. The tires grip race track surfaces even at high speeds. But stock car tires cannot grip wet tracks. For this reason, NASCAR officials will delay or cancel races when it rains.

Stock Car Interiors

Stock car interiors are the cabs where drivers sit. Stock car cabs have some devices that are similar to those in normal cars. But devices in stock car cabs are more sensitive than in normal cars. Stock car steering wheels are strong and work at very high speeds. Modified gas pedals help stock cars increase speed quickly. Sensitive brake pedals help drivers slow their stock cars down from very high speeds.

The interior of a stock car also has devices that a normal car interior usually does not have. A stock car has sensitive gauges that measure engine conditions. Gauges in stock cars take measurements of water temperature, oil pressure, and fuel pressure. Stock cars can break down if any of these gauges reads too high. Racers must closely watch the gauges when traveling at very high speeds.

Stock cars do not have some devices that ordinary cars have. For example, stock cars do not have speedometers. A speedometer shows how fast a car is traveling. This device is not necessary in stock cars since the racers try to drive as fast as possible. Stock cars do not have passenger seats. Stock cars also do not have radios that play music. Stock cars do have two-way radios that drivers use to talk to their racing teams.

The interior of a stock car has devices that a normal car does not have.

Concrete wall

Driver's cab

Exterior body

Wire fence

Safety net

WE CARE.

Wide tire

Chapter 4

Race organizers built the first pro stock car race tracks in the southeastern United States. Today, more than 40 major race tracks and many smaller tracks exist in the United States.

Each NASCAR track has its own qualities. Racers call the track in Bristol, Tennessee, "The World's Fastest Half Mile" because they can complete one lap quickly. Racers call Dover Downs "The Monster Mile" because many cars crash there. Many stock cars crash on the track in Darlington, South Carolina, too. Racers call this race track "Too Tough to Tame." The longest NASCAR Winston Cup Series race track is Talladega Superspeedway in Alabama. The shortest is Martinsville Speedway in Virginia.

Individuals or businesses usually own the race tracks. But NASCAR does own a few of the tracks. NASCAR also makes rules about the

The Martinsville Speedway in Virginia is the shortest NASCAR Winston Cup Series race track.

ways to build race tracks. NASCAR races can take place only on race tracks that NASCAR approves.

Race Track Size and Shape

Most NASCAR tracks are oval. The tracks have turns at two ends and long straightaways on two sides. A straightaway is a straight section of road. Spectators sit in grandstands around the outside of the tracks. The infield is the open area in the middle of the track. Racing crews set up their equipment in the infield.

NASCAR races also take place on two other kinds of tracks. These tracks are road-course tracks and tri-oval tracks. Road-course tracks have many right and left turns and only a few short straightaways. They are very difficult and dangerous for stock car racers. Tri-oval tracks are similar to oval tracks. But one side of the track curves out farther than the other. Tri-oval tracks look like large letter Ds.

NASCAR allows people to build two lengths of race tracks for the two types of races. Short tracks are less than one and one-half

---

The infield is the open area in the middle of a race track.

miles (2.4 kilometers) long. Tracks more than one and one-half miles long are superspeedways.

Race Tracks' Parts

Thick concrete walls surround NASCAR race tracks. Concrete is a hard surface made of sand, cement, and other materials. The walls protect spectators. Stock cars sometimes crash or run off the tracks. Walls keep the cars from going into the grandstands.

Wire fences are above the concrete walls. These fences are high and tilt in toward the track. The wire fences protect spectators from flying car parts during crashes.

NASCAR race tracks have either blacktop or concrete surfaces. Blacktop is the same material used to make ordinary roads. The turns on an oval NASCAR track are banked. Stock cars can travel at high speeds on banked turns. Racers must slow down to get around flat turns or they may crash their cars.

Every NASCAR track has a pit lane. A pit lane is a road that runs off the main track. Stock car racers drive into the pit lane for pit stops.

Thick concrete walls surround NASCAR race tracks to protect spectators.

Pit crews quickly check the stock cars, replace tires, and add gasoline during pit stops. Mechanics talk to the racers to find out if the cars need repairs.

NASCAR racing teams set up their equipment in the infield before races. They park their equipment trucks and trailers there. The trucks and trailers carry cars, parts, and tools from race to race.

Stock cars sometimes crash during races.

NASCAR Races

Between 30 and 45 stock cars take part in
NASCAR races today. The largest number of
racers to start a stock car race was 148. This
occurred in Daytona in 1953. Many races in
the 1950s had more than 80 racers. NASCAR
now limits the number of racers that can take
part in races.

NASCAR races can be very long. The
Daytona 500 is 500 miles (805 kilometers)

long. The World 600 at the Charlotte Motor Speedway is the longest NASCAR race. It lasts 600 miles (966 kilometers).

The racers line their cars up at a starting line at the beginning of a race. The race begins when the flagman waves a green flag. This racing official signals important moments in a race with flags. Stock cars sometimes crash during races. The flagman waves a yellow flag when there are hazards such as crashed cars on a race track.

The flagman uses flags of other colors to signal racers. A black flag signals a driver to the pit lane for a rule violation. A red flag signals that all cars should stop.

A white flag means there is only one lap left in the race. A checkered flag signals the end of the race. After the race, the winning racers take their cars to Victory Lane. Victory Lane is a road in the infield where winning racers collect their prizes.

Chapter 5

The People of Stock Car Racing

Stock car racers need to use their abilities when racing. They must have quick reflexes. Racers must move quickly to avoid hazards during races.

Stock car racers must learn to be patient. They need to wait for chances to move ahead of other cars. Racers concentrate on moving ahead during each lap of a long race. Races happen very quickly. Racers must pay close attention to everything in the race.

Racers must have stamina. This ability to keep performing a task for a long time helps racers during races. The longest NASCAR race is 600 miles (966 kilometers) long and takes more than four hours to complete.

NASCAR racers need upper-body strength. Their arms and chests must be strong enough to keep their cars under control. Stock cars

NASCAR racers wait for chances to move ahead of cars in front of them.

travel at speeds of more than 200 miles (322 kilometers) per hour. This makes it hard for racers to steer the cars. Racers must hold the steering wheels steady during fast turns.

Racing Crews
Pro stock car racing crews include mechanics and pit crew members. Mechanics build and repair the stock cars. They modify stock parts and fix engines so the cars have power. Mechanics know how to keep cars running at top speeds. Mechanics try to fix problems with stock cars quickly during races.

Pit crews change tires and fill gas tanks during races. Crews work very quickly. Every pit crew member has a certain job. One pit crew member lifts the car up with a jack. Another member removes the wheels. Another member puts new tires on the car. A final pit crew member fills the gas tank.

Racing Officials
Many racing officials work at NASCAR races. Besides the flagmen, race announcers describe

Pit crews work quickly to change tires and fill gas tanks during races.

racing action to spectators. Judges watch races to make sure racers follow NASCAR rules.

Racing judges also check stock cars before and after races. Judges can disqualify racers if their cars break NASCAR rules. Disqualified racers cannot take part in races.

Chapter 6

Pro Stock Car Safety

Pro stock cars have become safer since the early days of stock car racing. In the 1950s, stock cars had few safety devices in them. But those cars were not as fast as stock cars today. Stock cars now have many safety devices that protect racers during accidents.

Safety Devices

Several devices keep stock car drivers safe during accidents. Roll cages keep cars from collapsing on racers in crashes. Shatterproof windshields prevent broken glass from harming racers. Stock cars also have safety nets in the driver-side windows. The nets keep objects from flying inside and hitting the driver.

Stock cars in the 1950s had seat belts just like other cars. A stock car racer now wears a

Roll cages keep a car from collapsing on a racer during a crash.

complex seat belt called a five-point safety harness. Each five-point safety harness has five straps. Two straps come over the racer's shoulders. Another two fasten around the racer's sides. The fifth strap comes up between the racer's legs. The straps connect at the racer's waist.

Stock car gas tanks have rubber bladders inside them. The rubber bladders are large, strong bags that keep gas tanks from exploding during accidents. Racers also need to have fire extinguishers in their cars. Racers use fire extinguishers to spray chemicals that put out small fires.

Some safety devices make stock cars easier to control during crashes. Stock car tires have a special rubber lining. The lining prevents ripped or pierced tires from losing air. This way, racers can control their cars even if they have damaged tires.

Stock cars can easily flip over during an accident. Stock cars have flaps at the bottom of their windshields and on their roofs. These

Pro stock car racers wear a complex seatbelt called a five-point safety harness.

---

flaps stay flat during races. But the flaps pop up during accidents. The flaps catch the wind and keep the cars on the ground.

Racer Safety

Pro stock car racers must wear safety gear. The safety gear protects them from harm during accidents. Helmets, racing shoes, and gloves are part of racers' safety gear. Helmets

Pro stock car racers enjoy handling their powerful and fast stock cars.

protect racers' heads from shock during an accident. Racing shoes protect racers' feet. Gloves protect their hands.

Pro stock car racers must wear fire suits. These protective body suits resist fire. The fire suits cover all parts of the racers' bodies except their heads, feet, and hands. Some fire suits have water lines running through them.

Pumps send water through the water lines. The water keeps racers cool during long races.

Stock car racers must be in good condition to race. They must eat healthy meals and exercise. Racers must have plenty of sleep before races.

Pro stock car racers enjoy handling their powerful and fast stock cars. Racers say their sport is thrilling. The racers enjoy competing in stock car races for the chance to win prizes from NASCAR.

cab (KAB)—the area in a vehicle where a driver sits

chassis (CHASS-ee)—the frame on which a vehicle's body rests

fire extinguisher (FIRE ek-STING-gwish-ur)—a device that holds chemicals to spray on small fires

fire suit (FIRE SOOT)—a protective body suit that resists fire

flagman (FLAG-man)—a racing official who signals important moments in a race with flags

infield (IN-feeld)—the center of a race track

pit lane (PIT LAYN)—a road that runs off the main part of a race track; racers drive to the pit lane during races for pit stops.

road-course track (RHOD-KORSS TRAK)—a track that has many right and left turns and only a few short straightaways

roll cage (ROHL KAYJ)—a structure of strong metal tubing in a stock car that surrounds and protects stock car racers

short track (SHORT TRAK)—a race track that is less than one and one-half miles (2.4 kilometers) long

superspeedway (SOO-pur-speed-way)—a race track that is more than one and one-half miles (2.4 kilometers) long

suspension system (suh-SPEN-shuhn SISS-tuhm)—a system of springs and shock absorbers on a vehicle

tri-oval track (TRYE-OH-vuhl TRAK)—a near-oval race track with one side that curves out farther than the other

Victory Lane (VIK-tuh-ree LAYN)—a road in the infield where racers collect racing prizes

To Learn More

Benson, Michael. *Stock Car Spectacular.* New York: Crescent Books, 1995.

Burt, William M. *Behind the Scenes of NASCAR Racing.* Osceola, Wis.: Motorbooks International Publishers, 1997.

Golenbock, Peter. *American Zoom: Stock Car Racing—from the Dirt Tracks to Daytona.* New York: Macmillan USA, 1994.

Riley, Gail Blasser. *Top 10 NASCAR Drivers.* Hillside, N.J.: Enslow Publishing, 1995.

Useful Addresses

Daytona International Visitors Center
1801 West International Speedway Boulevard
Daytona Beach, FL 32114-1243

Motorsports Hall of Fame of America
43700 Expo Center Drive
Novi, MI 48375

NASCAR International
1310 Vindicator Street
Daytona Beach, FL 32114-1243

Internet Sites

Daytona USA
http://www.daytonausa.com

Motorsports Hall of Fame
http://www.mshf.com

NASCAR Online
http://www.nascar.com

Index